Nature's Children

PLATYPUS

Amanda Harman

GROLIER
EDUCATIONAL

FACTS IN BRIEF

Classification of Platypus

Class:	*Mammalia* (mammals)
Order:	*Monotremata* (monotremes)
Family:	*Ornithorhynchidae* (platypus family)
Genus:	*Ornithorhynchus*
Species:	*Ornithorhynchus anatinus* (platypus)

World distribution. Eastern Australia and Tasmania. Also introduced into Kangaroo Island in South Australia.

Habitat. Streams, rivers, and lakes, and their shores and banks.

Distinctive physical characteristics. Brown, furry, streamlined body; flattened from top to bottom; soft, rubbery bill, shaped like that of a duck; short limbs with webbed feet and long claws; broad, beaverlike tail.

Habits. A solitary animal that is mainly active at night; both in water and on land.

Diet. Aquatic insects, snails, mussels, shrimps, crayfish, earthworms, tadpoles and frogs, fish eggs, and small fish.

© 1999 Brown Partworks Limited
Printed and bound in U.S.A.
Editor: James Kinchen
Designer: Tim Brown
Reprinted in 2002

Published by:

GROLIER
EDUCATIONAL

Sherman Turnpike, Danbury, Connecticut 06816

Library of Congress Cataloging-in-Publishing Data

Platypus.
   p. cm. -- (Nature's children. Set 7)
   ISBN 0-7172-5543-3 (alk. paper) -- ISBN 0-7172-5531-X (set)
   1. Platypus--Juvenile Literature. [1. Platypus.] I. Grolier Educational (Firm) II. Series.

QL737.M72 P53 2001
599.2'9--dc21   00-067250

Contents

An Egg-laying Mammal   Page 6

Like a Mammal   Page 9

Like a Reptile   Page 10

Mr. and Mrs. Platypus   Page 13

Where Do They Live?   Page 14

In the Water   Page 17

On Land   Page 18

Shy Creatures   Page 21

Dinner Time   Page 22

An Amazing Bill   Page 24

Bulging Cheeks   Page 25

Saving Energy   Page 28

Fur Coat   Page 31

Sharing Territories   Page 32

Home Sweet Home   Page 35

Under Protection   Page 36

Danger from Pollution   Page 39

Springtime Breeding   Page 40

Nesting and Laying Eggs   Page 43

Baby Platypuses   Page 44

Puppy Play   Page 46

Words to Know   Page 47

Index   Page 48

The platypus is perhaps the strangest looking creature you will ever see. Imagine if someone put the bill and the webbed feet of a duck, the body of a large mole or small otter, and the tail of a beaver all together in one animal. The result would be the platypus. This creature looks so odd that when zoologists (scientists who study animals) first saw one, just over 200 years ago, they thought that someone was playing a big joke on them.

The name platypus comes from the Greek words for "flat footed" because of the animal's way of walking with its limbs stretched out flat on either side of the body. However, the platypus's appearance—along with its habit of swimming and diving in water—has meant that people call it by a whole range of other names. They include duck-billed platypus, duckbill, duck-mole, and water mole. Read this book to find out more about this strange but enchanting animal.

Opposite page: *With its ducklike bill, webbed feet, and fur-covered body, the platypus does not look like any other animal.*

An Egg-laying Mammal

There is only one species (type) of platypus alive today, although scientists believe that there may have been at least two other species in the distant past. That is because they have found two kinds of platypus fossil, one that is around 20 million years old, and one that is 85 million years old.

Like bears, cats, and humans, platypuses are mammals. However, platypuses are very unusual because they lay eggs. Almost every other mammal gives birth to live babies. There are just two other species of egg-laying mammal. Zoologists place them together with the platypus in a group called the monotremes. The other monotremes are the long-beaked spiny anteater, or echidna, found in New Guinea, and the short-beaked echidna, which is found in Australia and New Guinea. As their names suggest, these unusual creatures are covered in spines like those of a porcupine and have a beaklike nose.

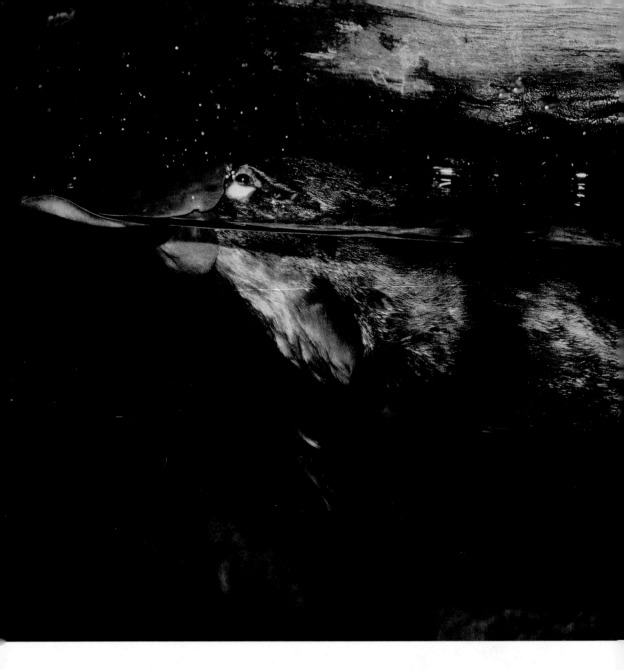

*This platypus's body temperature will stay the same
even if the water around it becomes very hot or cold.*

Like a Mammal

Along with their cousins the spiny anteaters, platypuses are probably the oldest mammals in the world. They have existed on Earth for around 150 million years! Animals that have been around and have not changed for such a long time are often called living fossils.

Zoologists call platypuses mammals because of three features that they have in common with other animals in this group. The first of them is a body covered with hair, or fur. The second of the platypus's mammal-like features is its habit of feeding its young with milk from its own body. The third characteristic that makes the platypus a mammal is the ability to keep its body at the same temperature.

Like a Reptile

Although platypuses are mammals, they have some features in common with reptiles, such as lizards and turtles. The most obvious of them is that they lay eggs. Like reptiles' eggs, platypus eggs are soft and flexible, and they feel a little like leather.

Another thing that platypuses have in common with reptiles is the small structure present on the end of the bill in newly hatched platypuses. It is called the egg tooth. It is used to tear open the eggshell during hatching. Platypuses also have parts of their skeleton that are very similar to those of reptiles. Their shoulders and hips are arranged so that platypuses walk with their legs out to the side. This is different from most mammals, which walk with their legs directly under their body. Like reptiles, but unlike mammals, platypuses have only one opening (called a cloaca) for getting rid of waste and for laying eggs. That is why platypuses are called monotremes, which means "one hole" in Greek.

The front legs of this platypus stick out on either side of its body. Platypuses walk like reptiles such as lizards and crocodiles.

Mr. and Mrs. Platypus

Female platypuses may grow to 22 inches (55 centimeters) long from the tip of their bill to the tip of their tail. They can weigh up to 3.5 pounds (1,600 grams). Males are a little larger than this, reaching a maximum length of 24 inches (60 centimeters) and a weight of 5 pounds (2,300 grams). This is about the size of a large rabbit. These measurements change with time of year and the area in which the platypuses live. Apart from size, the main way to tell the difference between a male and female platypus is to look for the sharp, pointed spike that is on the inside of the male's ankle. Be very careful, however, because it contains a strong venom that could hurt you and can even kill a smaller animal, such as a fox or a dog.

Opposite page:
Male platypuses use the venom from the sharp spike on their ankle to protect themselves if they are attacked by an enemy.

Where Do They Live?

Opposite page:
Platypuses make their homes along the banks of rivers and streams.

The platypus is found only along the eastern coast of Australia. It lives in an area that stretches from the city port of Townsville, Queensland, in the north, right down to the island of Tasmania in the south. Its favorite habitat for nesting is the shores of lakes or the rocky banks of rivers and streams. They may be found in warm, tropical regions or in cool areas, high in the mountains.

Like amphibians such as frogs and salamanders, the platypus is an amphibious creature. Although it is at home on land, it spends much of its time in the water.

The area shaded brown on this map shows where platypuses live.

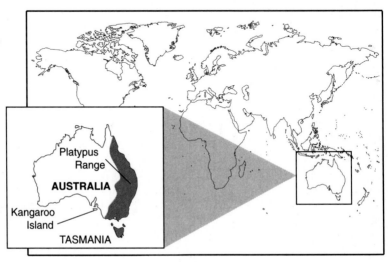

14

A platypus's streamlined body makes it very good at swimming and diving.

In the Water

Platypuses are extremely well designed for life in the water. Their body is flattened and streamlined, so they cut through the water very easily. That is very useful, especially when diving down to the river- or lake bed. They are able to dive for as long as 14 minutes before they have to return to the surface of the water to breathe in air. However, most dives only last for around a minute.

The platypuses' thick, yellowish or reddish brown fur is made up of two layers, making it totally waterproof. The webbing on their feet is a great help, too: it grows past the claws to form large paddles. The webbing is biggest on the front paws, which the platypus uses to pull it through the water. The hind paws have less webbing and are used, along with the broad tail, for steering. That is another very unusual feature for a mammal. Other water-loving mammals, such as otters and seals, use mainly their back legs to push themselves along when they are swimming.

On Land

Platypuses are much less comfortable on land than they are in the water. They walk on their "knuckles," turning their toes under and folding back the webbing so that it does not get damaged. The way their legs stick out at right angles from their body also makes it difficult for platypuses to make their way across the ground. They cannot run and can only waddle along clumsily like a duck.

Platypuses are easily caught by their enemies when they are on land. The main enemies of platypuses are carnivorous (meat-eating) mammals, such as foxes and domestic dogs and cats. However, some birds of prey, large fish, and reptiles, such as snakes and crocodiles, will also have a platypus for dinner.

This platypus will find it much more difficult to get around once he has climbed out of the water.

Shy Creatures

The platypus is a shy creature and is very rarely seen by humans. It spends most of the day in its burrow, only coming out to feed in the evening and through the night. That makes it an extremely difficult animal to study, and scientists still have lots to learn about this fascinating creature. The only way you would know if a platypus had been close by would be a loud splash as it dived underwater. "Splash diving" allows the platypus to escape from its enemies quickly. The noise of the splash sometimes startles the enemies, and the platypus can get away.

Opposite page:
If you surprise a platypus when it is on land, it will quickly dive into the water to get away from you.

Dinner Time

Opposite page: *Platypuses hunt for food among rocks and mud on the bottom of lakes or rivers.*

The platypus is a carnivorous animal, feeding on a whole range of creatures that live in the water. During the summer the main part of the platypus diet is made up of water insects and their larvae (young). During the winter, when there aren't many insects around, the platypus may catch and eat earthworms, snails, mussels, shrimp, crayfish, tadpoles, frogs, fish eggs, and small fish. Platypuses have a very large appetite and eat almost their own weight in food every day. If your appetite was as big as that of a platypus, you would have to eat more than 450 hamburgers every day.

In order to feed, the platypus dives into the lake or river and swims along the bottom. It moves its head from side to side and probes the mud for food with its bill. When it dives, it closes its eyes, ears, and nostrils, so it cannot really see, hear, or smell anything. So how does the platypus avoid bumping into things? And—even more importantly—how does it find its food?

An Amazing Bill

The platypus can avoid bumping into obstacles and find its food in the water because of its amazing bill. Unlike that of a duck or other bird, the platypus's bill is extremely soft and flexible, and very sensitive to touch. Even more important than this, however, is the fact that it is covered in thousands of tiny sense organs that can detect electricity. Very weak electric currents are given off by most objects—especially by the muscles of animals as they move. So the platypus's rubbery bill acts as a kind of extra pair of "eyes." The platypus can use it to find out where things are and where in the mud to find moving prey. This means that platypuses have no problem catching prey when the water is dark and muddy. It also means that platypuses can find their way around underwater even at nighttime.

Bulging Cheeks

As the platypus sifts through the sand, gravel, and mud on the bed of the river or lake, it stores any food it finds in its cheek pouches. Platypuses have two of them, one on each side of its mouth, just like a hamster. When the cheek pouches are full, or when the platypus needs to breathe, it rises to the surface of the water and takes the food out of the pouches. It does this with two tiny toothlike projections that are far back on its tongue.

Adult platypuses do not have actual teeth. Instead, they have tough plates made from a material a bit like that in cows' horns. They allow platypuses to crush and grind their food into tiny pieces. Before swallowing it, they pass any waste material, such as bits of shell and bone, along tiny grooves on the edges of their lower jaw and spit it out into the water.

Saving Energy

Opposite page:
*A platypus saves
energy by storing it
up as fat in its tail.
This fat can then
be used by the
animal when there
is a shortage of
food in the winter.*

Like other mammals, the platypus has the remarkable ability to keep its body temperature at a certain level. However, this level is much lower than for most other mammals—around 90°F (32°C), rather than around 98°F (37°C), which is what your body temperature is. The fact that the platypus's body temperature is so low probably saves it a lot of energy when the weather gets cold.

Another way a platypus saves energy and keeps warm in winter is by having a thick fur coat. It can work as insulation in freezing water only if the platypus keeps it clean and waterproof. So to keep it clean, the platypus "combs" it regularly with the claws on its back feet and with its bill.

The platypus's fur coat is even thicker than that of a polar bear! It helps the platypus stay warm in the cold winter months.

Fur Coat

The platypus's fur coat is very good at keeping it warm because it is made up of two different layers that trap warm air between them. First there is a layer of fine, densely packed underfur, which contains at least 3,600 hairs to every square inch (600 hairs to every square centimeter) of skin. On top of this undercoat is a layer of longer fur called guard hairs. Each of these guard hairs is over a half-inch (17 millimeters) long. The underside of the platypus's tail is completely naked, and it gets cold when the platypus is sleeping. To keep this from happening, the platypus curls up with its tail snug against the thick fur on its belly.

With such a warm fur coat the platypus can easily get too hot during the summer. The cool water and underground burrows help prevent the platypus from getting too hot at this time. In addition, the platypus molts all its fur and gradually grows a new coat every summer.

Sharing Territories

The platypus is a lonely animal, preferring to nest and feed by itself. Platypus families generally consist of a female and her young. The platypus is also a territorial creature and may wander along the same route every night, covering a distance of up to several miles at one time. Platypus territories often overlap, however, and over time as many as five individuals may share a patch of suitable habitat around a stretch of clean water.

Usually at the center of a platypus's territory is its burrow. It has an entrance by the water's edge at least partially hidden from enemies by rocks, vegetation, or fallen logs. Sometimes one individual will have more than one burrow, and occasionally two platypuses will share a burrow.

Home Sweet Home

A platypus's burrow consists of a narrow tunnel winding for 3 to 10 feet (1 to 3 meters). The burrow ends in a small cave where the platypus sleeps for up to 17 hours every day. The tunnel usually points upward so that the cave is well above the water level. This means that the sleeping platypus will not drown if the river or lake rises during a flood.

The platypus's strong, stout limbs, with their long claws, are perfect for digging the tunnels and caves. The animal digs rapidly with its front paws and shovels the soil underneath its body so that it piles up behind. As well as hiding the entrance to its burrow, the platypus may also block the tunnel with earth at certain points. That is to keep its enemies from entering the platypus's home and having it for dinner.

Opposite page: *Platypuses often enter their burrows through underground openings. The burrow itself is always well above the water line.*

Under Protection

In the past many people hunted platypuses for their meat, as well as for their soft, glossy fur. They also collected them for natural history displays because the animals look so strange. As a result, the numbers of this fascinating Australian species began to fall, and the platypus nearly became extinct. During the 20th century, however, laws were passed to protect the platypus, and there are now lots of them throughout most of its range. For example, in the Australian state of Victoria there are 31 different river systems, and the platypus is found in as many as 26 of them. Despite this fact, many people believe that the platypus is still rare. The reason for this is simply that it is a very shy animal that hides away in its burrow during the day. So you would have to be very lucky indeed to see one out in the wild.

Danger from Pollution

Although the platypus is common and there are lots of them in Australia, zoologists still think it could be endangered, especially in areas around large cities. For example, the platypus is still rare around the city of Melbourne. The main danger to the platypus today comes from humans. Because humans are polluting the platypus's home, the animals often drown by becoming caught up in litter and abandoned fishing nets. In 1994 the Australian Platypus Conservancy was set up so that scientists could learn all about this amazing creature and discover exactly what it needs to survive. The organization has also set up campaigns to tell people about the platypus and to teach them to keep their environment clean and free of litter.

Opposite page:
This platypus drowned because it became tangled in a fishing net.

Springtime Breeding

Platypuses do all their courting and mating in one particular season of the year. Like many animals, it is in the springtime. At this time the venom in the male's ankle spurs becomes especially powerful. A male may use these venomous spikes to fight with other males for his right to mate with a female. For all his showing off, however, it is the female who actually decides which of the males she will take as her partner.

When she is ready, the female platypus performs a kind of courtship dance in the water, aimed at the male as he rests at the water's surface. During this "dance" she swims toward him until the two animals are face to face and touches him with her bill for up to 10 minutes. She may also rub her bill along his side and dive below him, swimming up and brushing her belly against his belly. Eventually the male responds to her advances, and they will then mate in the water.

Platypus females work very hard to dig out their burrow and collect material to insulate the nest.

Nesting and Laying Eggs

Before the female lays her eggs, she gets busy digging an especially long passage in her burrow. This long tunnel may wind uphill for up to 100 feet (30 meters). At the end of the tunnel the female digs out an incubation nest. She then lines the nest with grass, plant roots, and leaves that she has gathered. She carries them to the nest by wrapping them up under her tail, which she holds beneath her belly.

Once the nest is finished, the female platypus curls up so that she forms a tiny incubation pouch between her belly and her tail. She lays between one and three round, white eggs. These eggs are the size of robins' eggs but are soft and tacky. They stick to each other and also to the fur on the mother's belly.

Baby Platypuses

Opposite page: *Platypuses will stay with their mother until they are at least one year old, when they leave to set up on their own.*

The leathery eggs remain stuck to their mother's fur for the next 8 to 12 days, incubating in the hot air trapped in the incubation pouch formed by her curled-up body. Eventually the young babies break their way out of the eggs using the egg tooth on the end of their bill. Right after they have hatched from the eggs, baby platypuses are less than an inch (2.5 centimeters) long.

Once out of the egg, they begin the long journey through their mother's hair to the milk glands on her belly. Unlike other mammals, platypuses do not have specialized teats for suckling their young. Instead, the milk oozes from tiny holes in the mother's skin, and the babies lap it up from tufts of fur. They do this until they are old and strong enough to survive on their own. Then the nest will be their home for the next four or five months, while their mother leaves the burrow every so often and returns with food.

Puppy Play

While they are growing up, the young platypuses often fool around together like puppies playing. They wrestle each other down to the ground and roll over together on the bank or in the water, biting at each other with their bill and raising their front paws playfully.

Zoologists do not know exactly how old platypuses are when they become adults and are able to breed with other platypuses. However, they think that the males' venom spur has grown to its final size when he is about one year old, and that this is when the platypus becomes an adult. It is also a mystery how long platypuses live in the wild. One male lived as long as 17 years in a zoo!

Words to Know

Amphibious Able to live both on land and in the water.

Aquatic Living in water.

Carnivore An animal that feeds mainly on other animals.

Courtship The process animals use to decide who they will mate with.

Egg tooth A toothlike point used to help a baby animal crack its way out of an egg.

Extinct When all of the animals of a particular species have died, and there are no more left anywhere in the world.

Fossil Any remains of an animal from long ago that have been preserved in stone.

Gland A part of an animal that produces a fluid. In female mammals it is a type of gland that produces milk.

Incubate To keep eggs warm so that they will hatch.

Mate To come together to produce young.

Molt Shedding old skin, fur, or feathers to make way for new.

Teat The raised part on a female mammal's breast that gives out milk for her young to drink.

Territory Area where an animal hunts or breeds, which it defends against other animals.

Zoologist A scientist who studies animals.

INDEX

amphibian, 14, 47

bill, 5, 10, 13, 22, 24, 28, 40,
   44, 46; *illus.*, 45
body temperature, 9, 28
burrow, 21, 31, 32, 35, 36, 43, 44;
   illus., 34

carnivore, 18, 22, 47
cheek pouches, 25

digging, 35
diving, 5, 17, 21, 22; *illus.*, 20

echidna, 6; *illus.*, 7
eggs, 6, 10, 43, 44
egg tooth, 10, 44, 47
electricity, 24
enemies, 18, 21, 32, 35
extinct, 36, 39, 47

feeding, 9, 22, 24, 32; *illus.*, 23
fossil, 6, 9, 47
fur, 5, 9, 10, 17, 28, 31, 36, 44

gland, 44, 47

hair, 9, 31, 44

hatching, 10, 44

incubate, 43, 44, 47

mammal, 6, 9, 10, 17, 18, 28,
   36
mating, 40, 47
milk, 9, 44
molt, 31, 47
monotreme, 6, 10

nest, 43, 44

pollution, 3, 39
prey, 18, 24

reptiles, 10

tail, 5, 13, 17, 28, 31, 43
teat, 44, 47
territory, 32, 47

venom, 13, 40, 46

webbing, 5, 17, 18; *illus.*, 4

zoologist, 5, 6, 39, 46, 47

Cover Photo: Dave Watts / NHPA
Photo Credits: Dave Watts / NHPA, pages 4, 12, 15, 19, 20, 26&27, 45; Tom Brakefield /
Corbis, page 7; Australian Picture Library / Corbis, page 8, 33; Paul R Wilkinson / Bruce
Coleman, page 11; Klein/Hubert / Still Pictures, page 16, 29; Joe McDonald / Corbis, pages
23, 42; Bruce Coleman, page 30; Martin Harvey / NHPA, page 34; Bruce Coleman / Bruce
Coleman page 37; A.N.T. / NHPA, page 38; Norbert Wu / NHPA, page 41.